ARMED FORCES
★ ★ ★
Army

NIGHT STALKERS

by Carlos Alvarez

TORQUE
TM

BELLWETHER MEDIA ★ MINNEAPOLIS, MN

Library of Congress
Alvarez, Carlos, 1968–
  Army Night Stalkers / by Carlos Alvarez.
      p. cm. — (Torque : Armed Forces)
  Summary: "Amazing photography accompanies engaging
information about the Army Night Stalkers. The combination
of high-interest subject matter and light text is intended for
students in grades 3 through 7"—Provided by publisher.
  Includes bibliographical references and index.
  ISBN 978-1-60014-280-2 (hardcover : alk. paper)
  1. United States. Army. Special Operations Aviation Regiment
(Airborne), 160th—Juvenile literature. 2. Night and all-weather
operations (Military aeronautics)—United States—Juvenile
literature. 3. Military helicopters—United States—Juvenile
literature. I. Title.
  UG1233.A46 2010
  358.4—dc22   2009008495

030110   1160

CONTENTS

★ ★ ★

★ ★ ★

Chapter One

WHAT ARE ARMY NIGHT STALKERS?

The United States Army's Night Stalkers are a highly trained team of helicopter pilots. They are also known as the 160th Special Operations Aviation **Regiment** (Airborne). The Army formed the Night Stalkers in 1981.

The military needed an elite group of helicopter pilots to take on dangerous **missions**. Today, the Night Stalkers are the U.S. military's best helicopter support unit.

Night Stalkers use helicopters to perform quick, secret missions. They drop off special operations forces behind enemy lines. They also pick them up. Night Stalkers bring supplies to these forces and sometimes carry out attacks on enemy targets. Night Stalkers fly their helicopters fast and low to the ground. They perform most of their missions at night. The darkness helps them hide from the enemy.

Chapter Two

WEAPONS AND GEAR

Night Stalkers use many types of helicopters to complete missions. One of them is the MH-60 Black Hawk. They use it to sneak behind enemy lines and supply troops. Night Stalkers use the MH-6 Little Bird for **reconnaissance** missions. The CH-47 Chinook is their best **cargo** and transport helicopter.

CH-47 Chinook

Most Night Stalker helicopters are armed with weapons. Some have 7.62mm **miniguns**. These guns can fire up to 6,000 rounds per minute. Powerful 70mm rocket pods can blast through enemy armor. Some helicopters even carry guided air-to-ground **missiles**.

MH-60 Black Hawk

Night-vision goggles

Night Stalker pilots need gear for night missions. Some aircraft have special night-vision systems. These help them see at night. Pilots can also wear **night-vision goggles**. Pilots **navigate** in the dark using a **global positioning system (GPS)**.

The Night Stalkers
are based out of Fort
Campbell in Kentucky.

Chapter Three

LIFE AS A NIGHT STALKER

Pilots need to go through intense training to become Night Stalkers. They must have 1,000 flight hours. At least 100 hours must be done with night-vision goggles. Pilots must also pass physical and mental tests.

Night Stalkers start with a "basic mission qualified" status. They cannot command a mission until they have 12 to 18 months experience. They are then "fully mission qualified."

The trainees who pass join the Green Platoon. They then have 14 more weeks of training. It starts with three weeks of survival training. Recruits then take classes on combat and aviation. Next, recruits spend two weeks learning about navigation. Finally, they spend six weeks learning to fly a specific helicopter. This is the type of helicopter they will fly on missions.

Both men and women can become Night Stalkers. Women are allowed to serve only in staff roles. They cannot serve in direct combat.

Green Platoon members who complete their training get assignments. They take their posts in the 160th Special Operations Aviation Regiment. They are assigned to Night Stalker headquarters or to one of four **battalions**. They then join a **company**. Each company is ready to **deploy** within four hours. They try to live up to their motto: "Anywhere, anytime, Night Stalkers don't quit!"

★ ★ ★

battalion—an army unit usually consisting of a headquarters and three or more companies

cargo—the goods carried by a vehicle

company—a subdivision of a battalion

deploy—to be sent on a military mission

global positioning system (GPS)—a device that uses satellites orbiting Earth to determine a precise position on the globe

minigun—a multi-barreled machine gun with a very high rate of fire

missile—an explosive launched at targets on the ground or in the air

mission—a military task

navigate—to find one's way in unfamiliar terrain

night-vision goggles—a special set of glasses that allow the wearer to see at night

reconnaissance—secret observation

regiment—a military division composed of a number of battalions

TO LEARN MORE

★ ★ ★

AT THE LIBRARY

David, Jack. *United States Army*. Minneapolis, Minn.: Bellwether, 2008.

Hopkins, Ellen. *U.S. Special Operations Forces*. Chicago, Ill.: Heinemann, 2004.

Weiser, Andrea L. *U.S. Army Special Operations Command: Night Stalkers Special Operations Aviation*. Mankato, Minn.: Capstone, 2000.

ON THE WEB

Learning more about the Night Stalkers is as easy as 1, 2, 3.

1. Go to www.factsurfer.com.

2. Enter "Night Stalkers" into the search box.

3. Click the "Surf" button and you will see a list of related Web sites.

With factsurfer.com, finding more information is just a click away.

INDEX

★ ★ ★